THE COINS OF THE CENTRAL AMERICAN FEDERATION

BY

JOSE A. MEJIA

Copyright 2011 Jose A Mejia
All Rights Reserved.
ISBN-13:978-0615570181
ISBN-10:0615570186

Please visit our websites to learn more
www.centralamericancoins.com

www.alliancelimitedcollectibles.com

Also by Jose A. Mejia

The Numismatic History of El Salvador

Contents

Chapter 1: Introduction

Chapter 2: Independence and Annexation 1821-1823

Chapter 3: The Federation Is Created

Chapter 4: The Federal Coins

Chapter 5: Chaos: The Arce Presidency and Civil War

Chapter 6: The Liberal Way

Chapter 7: Cultural Clash: The Decline of the Liberals and the Federation

Chapter 8: Coins After the Collapse of the Federation

Chapter 9: Legacy of Union

Chapter 10: The Legacy of the CAF Designs

Chapter 11: The Central American Federation Coins

Chapter 12: Collecting Central American Federation Coins

Bibliography

Chapter 1: Introduction

Chapter 1: Introduction

It's hard to believe that at one point in time Central America was part of a kingdom and later an empire. However, most people are more surprised to find out that these individual countries were once a united country known as the Federation.

The nations that encompass Central America (with the exception of Panama and Belize) in the modern era: Guatemala, Nicaragua, El Salvador, Honduras, and Costa Rica were all states in the nation that was once known as the Central American Federation. This institution was created in 1823 and lasted until till 1839. The Federation had many goals to emulate the United States and French constitutions, however, unlike these nations, the Federation was so divided that any policies made were impossible to enforce in all states. Problems ranging from poverty to illiteracy made any reform impossible to achieve, and personal interest eroded the Federation.

However, in the short two decades of its existence, the Federation minted some of the most beautiful silver and gold pieces in Latin America. Although these coins were minted in various states, Guatemala's mint became the most active of the era. However, depending on one mint, in the most conservative state of the Federation, created major political problems that led to shortages of coins throughout the country.

The political instabilities and various civil wars that plagued the Federation brought to the forefront the usage of provincial coins and foreign coins in the marketplace when the federal mints stopped producing them. Eventually, countermarks were developed in various states to differentiate these coins, but ultimately, depending on foreign coins and provincial coins made running the federal economy a nightmare for the leaders of the nation. In essence, it became a daily reminder to citizens that the federal authorities were incompetent and that they were better off depending on their own state for support.

The Federation ended with General Francisco Morazán's death in 1842. Nevertheless, the five states all waited and hoped for a new entity to replace the Federation. However, in 1847 the establishment of a republic in Guatemala ended any hope of a new union. In the late nineteen century many leaders contemplated a re-establishment of a union, but by the twenty century those thoughts had been replaced with creating an economic union via free trade agreements.

Having a united Central America, even if only in free trade, is still a dream of many Liberals. Let us hope that they will learn from the mistakes of the old Central American Federation to create a stronger economic environment for this impoverished region to prosper and achieve its potential in the twenty first century.

Coins During Colonial Times

The states that comprise Central America by the late eighteen century had been administered into a new region called the Kingdom of Guatemala by the Spanish government. The many Spanish reforms, by the monarchy, had finally led to this region controlling its own destiny without too much influence from Mexico City. Or at least, that was the theory behind the new kingdom. In reality, much of Central America had been forgotten by the Spanish government and many major decisions still had to go through the Mexican vice regency.

Ever since its discovery by Columbus and the various explorers who founded many cities in Central America, the region had depended on Spanish colonial coins from the new world. However, the local authorities were given the power in 1731 to establish a mint in Guatemala City, which they did in 1733. Other cities like, Tegucigalpa, had formally petitioned the Spanish colonial authorities all the way back to 1714, but had been denied the authority to establish a mint.

The Guatemalan mint would produce several different coins and would have the G or NG mintmark depending on the year of production. The most common types of coins minted and available were the pillar type and bust coins. However, due to the low quality of the dies, many of these coins resembled cobs.

Nonetheless, the mint didn't satisfy the needs of the kingdom and many coins from throughout the Americas circulated freely. The lack of coins would continue to haunt Central America until well into the twenty century.

The Mayan Calendar

Chapter 2: Independence and Annexation 1821-1823

Chapter 2 Independence and Annexation 1821-1823

The turmoil in Spain and the many revolutions taking place in Mexico and South America had not taken hold of the leaders of Central America. In fact, when the Spanish empire fell in Mexico, many citizens had no idea that the crown no longer held power in most of Latin America. The rumors of independence led many intellectuals and elites to finally come together and declare independence on September 15, 1821.

Although, independence was achieved peacefully, the cause of disunity and lack of identity once the states united to form the Federation has been debated. The question of identity became the very root of political discourse after independence was declared. Many of the elites and the majority of the former Spanish administrators resided in Guatemala City. The other states feared a stronger Guatemala, and many feared that any state or republic founded with Guatemala City as the capital would never happen.

Why so much hostility to Guatemala City? Well, the capital of the old kingdom had enjoyed many luxuries. Many farmers and business men, for example, had no choice under Spanish rule, but to take out loans from merchants or apply for licenses which always were based out of Guatemala. This sense of injustice made many elites in the other states wary of a union with a state they felt was more hostile than Spain itself. Many elites wanted a new monarch or Spanish Republic founded in the new world to replace Spain. Anything was better than to join Guatemala. Thus, the idea to join the new Mexican empire started to take root in the former states of the Kingdom of Guatemala

It took many months for the intellectuals of the region to exchange conventions and ideas. Not much happened during the first few months of independence. Therefore, the new independent states continued to use many of the same coins they had previously. However, new coins from Mexico and South America also started to appear and were used during the first few years of independence. Furthermore, once the idea of joining Mexico came into play, a few interesting pieces started to circulate in the region, advocating the new empire.

The Honduras Coins

Agustin Emperor 1823 Coins

The delegation that left Central America for Mexico to seek an audience with Emperor Iturbide included a few delegates from the state of Honduras. This delegation was successful in getting the, authority or blessing, if you will, to start a mint in order to aid in meeting the state's expenses.

The mint was established in the city of Comayagua and started producing coins featuring Emperor Iturbide with 1823 dates on them. The small mint produced 1 and 2 *reales* coins in silver honoring the new emperor. These coins circulated in Honduras and in nearby states.

However, the coins with Iturbide's bust became scarce and were in a matter of months out of the market. The lack of die details on the coins and the fact that many people seemed to prefer the older Spanish style colonial coins made the authorities abandon the Iturbide design for the traditional Roman numeral designs.

Tegucigalpas

Probably, the most common Honduran coin minted and circulated after independence, was the so called *Tegucigalpas*. These coins were minted in silver with denominations of 1 and 2 *reales*.

These coins would vary and many would be used as cobs coins. In fact, the lack of coins in the Federation would see these coins being used in the market causing future states to pass laws trying to ban them, because of the ease of counterfeiting them.

Outside of these two sets of coins minted by Honduras, no other state minted official coins for circulation after independence and before the creation of the Federation. Both Costa Rica and Nicaragua minted cob coins in provisional mints. Guatemala, though, did mint a few medallions commemorating Emperor Iturbide.

Ironically, most of the Guatemalan elite wanted to join Mexico in order to keep their social standing and to open new markets to their goods. Most of the Liberal intellectuals were dead set against any Mexican union in most states. However, only the state of San Salvador had a majority of leaders who openly opposed any integration with Mexico. In fact, they drafted a letter to Washington, DC, and asked to join the United States as a state. Such strategies were organized in order to stop the Mexican emperor Iturbide from trying to annex the entire region.

Unfortunately, in 1822 Emperor Iturbide sent General Filisola to run his new territory and Filisola quickly went to San Salvador to squash the resistance in the state and to impose Iturbide's role in the region. Although General Filisola was confident about controlling Central America, the political instability of Mexico made him wary of a permanent stay in the region.

By 1823, the First Mexican Empire of Iturbide had collapsed. General Filisola was recalled to Mexico. Although, General Filisola was seen by many Central Americans as the enemy, the general treated many of the leaders of the region equally. So, instead of leading his army back to Mexico as quickly as he could, he stopped in Guatemala City and organized a new convention to decide the future of the region.

The convention of 1823 took months to come to terms in establishing a new nation. The convention was finally organized on July 1, 1823, and quickly declared their independence from Mexico. The United Provinces of Central America was created soon afterward.

The dissolution of the first Mexican Empire would have two immediate impacts on Central America. First, the state of Chiapas, once a part of Guatemala, chose to join the state of Mexico. Second, the cost of maintaining General Filisola's troops and the cost of sending them back to Mexico would eventually bankrupt the Guatemalan treasury and make the management of the new nation extremely difficult.

Agustin de Iturbide

Chapter 3 The Federation Is Born

Chapter 3 The Federation Is Born

The Federation was finally established on November 22, 1824. The country has also been referred to as the United Provinces of Central America, since that was the title the region was under shortly after independence from Mexico.

The first congress had to decide how to divide the congressional seats for all states in the Federation. The last known census had taken place in 1821 and had shown a population of 1,270,000. Therefore, it was decided that each congressional representative represented 30,000 citizens. The breakdown of representatives by state was as follows: Guatemala ,18, San Salvador, 9, Honduras, 6, Nicaragua ,6, and Costa Rica, 2. The congressional representatives were evenly divided among the population, but no one could argue that Guatemala, having the most representatives, would influence the actions of both the congress and the president.

Another problem the Federation had was the unequal representation of minorities in the union. Although, Guatemala's elite controlled the region, most of them were either white or mestizo and few were Indian. Ironically, Guatemala had, and still has, the highest proportion of Mayan Indians in Central America. These citizens lived on the outskirts of the capital and generally didn't get involved in politics. However, tensions were always high between the elite and the Indian population regardless of whether Liberals or Conservatives were in power; this was because of economic policies alienated the Indian population. Other races included blacks' totaling 20,000 and whites 100,000, most of these groups were spread throughout the various states.

Ironically, Costa Rica, which had a majority of white and mestizo population, didn't have many issues with the indigenous population, mainly because the state rarely was impacted by federal policy. The long distance and isolation by federal authorities made it easy for Costa Rica to adopt its own laws and policies and to simply reject federal laws. This isolation would spare Costa Rica the civil wars the Federation would have, and their human and economic cost.

Many problems cast a cloud on the young nation. First, the new nation was essentially bankrupt. The Mexican army had cost the state most of its wealth, and in order to run the new nation a loan was needed. The British banking house of Barclays, Herring and Richardson, was the most interested creditors, and soon gave the Federation a loan of 5,000,000 pesos, although the nominal value of the loan was 7,142,047 pesos. This loan came with a 6 percent interest rate and was to be repaid in 20 years. The loan had been agreed upon by the first president of the Federation, a Salvadoran Liberal general named Jose Arce. However, President Arce's term was clouded with so much hostility and corruption, that he failed to use the loan in a positive way and instead used it to fund the government's first civil war.

Provisional Mints

Prior to the first monetary law passed by the Federation in 1824, several states had set up their own provincial mint to produce cob coins. Honduras, Nicaragua and Costa Rica minted and countermarked a number of cob coins that circulated in their respective states.

The Honduran provincial mints started shortly after Deputy Don Joaquin Lindo bought a coinage press and started producing coins in the covenant of San Francisco by March of 1823. Around the same time, the provincial mint of Comayagua also started producing cobs and would remain active until 1825. By that time, the state had created some unique silver coins that resembled federally issued coins, which led to the federal authority's closure of the mint to bring the equipment up to its standards.

Nicaragua minted several cob coins for local usage prior to 1824. However, the provincial cob mints didn't possess the equipment necessary to expand and mint coins. Thus, shortly after the federal monetary law was approved, the state ceased minting cob coins and would rely mostly on federal and foreign coins for most of its need.

In the case of Costa Rica, the discovery of mines in the region of Montes del Aguacante led to a push by authorities to establish a mint. In fact, the state passed a monetary law on May 10, 1823 to regulate the minting of coins. However, we have only drawings of the proposed coins, since none were ever minted. The provisional mint started producing coins right after the federal congress approved plans to make a federal mint in Costa Rica. This led to some unique gold coins being minted in 1825 that resembled federal coins. This violation of federal law and the lack of detailed dies led federal authorities to close both Honduran and Costa Rican mints for several years in order to bring them up to code.

The Two Party System

Political instability is not something new in Latin America. Although many leaders had different schools of thoughts and didn't agree with their counterparts, the majority of political leaders fell into either the Liberal or Conservative parties of the region.

The Liberal party advocated: free trade, a division of church and state, universal education, and a united central government. The Conservative party, on the other hand, wanted to have a strong church state, decentralized government, regulated commerce and to keep the status quo. In essence, the Liberals wanted to radically change Central America in the same light as the United States, while the Conservatives wanted to keep a system of government that resembled the old Spanish empire.

Although, it was the Conservatives that pushed hard to be annexed by Mexico, the Liberal party took up the fight for a united Central America. When Emperor Iturbide fell, the credibility of the elite Conservatives fell too. The Liberals took this opportunity to elect a congress and president that they felt served and reflected the needs of the new nation. From the start, this political rivalry would destroy the nation's progress.

The first congress that assembled in 1823 had a major problem on their hands. The majority of its leaders wanted a capital and a federal district, but they had assembled in Guatemala, the old stronghold capital of the colonial elite that had favored Spanish and Mexican autonomy. Naturally, most of the intellectuals of the time distrusted the old Guatemalan elite and felt that no laws would pass due to the influence of the old elite. However, Guatemala had both the majority of the nation citizen's and the majority of its wealth too. Thus, the congressional members were stuck in a capital they felt undermined the new nation, yet was vital to keeping the nation united.

During the first few years a committee of political leaders led the nation. During 1823, the first central committee ran the nation. Its purpose was to guide and organize the states after the Independence from Mexico. The second committee would run the nation from the end of 1823 until elections in 1825. This committee set the ground for establishing the main responsibilities of government, ranging from elections to establishing a supreme court.

However, compromises were made in many fundamental agencies of government that would hamper the power of the future president of the republic. For example, states were given the right to collect certain taxes within their borders, but they would in turn have to deliver the majority of the income to the federal government. Of course, many states chose to undercut the federal authorities by keeping a large portion of tax revenues. In another example, Costa Rica, predicting that it would be neglected by federal authorities, negotiated a commercial pact with Honduras in 1824. The push for states' rights made a united federal government only a concept even in practice.

Catholicism had always been a major issue among colonial Latin Americans. Guatemala, having the largest population, was awarded by the crown an archbishop's post. When independence came, many of the citizens of the other states wanted to establish an archbishop in their state, regardless of whether it was approved by the state or the Church. An independent archbishop was seen as a symbol of independence. San Salvador and Bishop Miguel Delgado made a strong push for an archbishop post since; the state had the second largest population in the new Federation. The competition among different states to establish an independent archbishop post clearly suggested that the states in the federation couldn't even agree on church procedure, even though they were for the most part Catholic.

The federal army was another problem. Since the nation had an all volunteer army, the federal government had to rely heavily on Guatemala's militias. However, all the states in the Federation had major militias whose responsibilities were to govern and protect the state. Thus, in many of the wars fought by the federal authorities, troop shortages were a major issue and ultimately spelled doom to whoever was president at that time.

President Arce

The political situation in congress didn't improve much, either. When the time came to elect the country's first president both sides advocated for their choice. The Liberals supported Salvadoran General Jose Manuel Arce, while the Conservative supported the former mayor of Guatemala, Jose Cecilio Del Valle. The elections were controversial, since in the end the loser of the elections was elected president with the support of congress.

President Jose Manuel Arce

Historians agree that the elections were won by Del Valle. However, congress felt a recount was needed. The Liberal majority in congress awarded the presidency to Arce. Jose Del Valle retired from politics and went back to writing and teaching. What would have happened if Valle had become president? Honestly, Del Valle might have avoided a civil war and bloodshed; however, it's highly unlikely that he would have changed much of the political or economic structure of the Federation. Nevertheless, President Manual Arce took office on April 29, 1825, as the first president of the Central American Federation.

Senator Jose Del Valle

Chapter 4: The Federal Coins

Chapter 4: The Federal Coins

The second national congress passed a monetary law on March 19, 1824. This law regulated the size and monetary unit of each coin minted by the state. The monetary law had seven decrees:

Decree 1: All coins were prohibited from being minted with any Spanish insignia.

Decree 2: All silver and gold coins minted followed the Spanish monetary units.

Decree 3: On the bust of all silver coins, five volcanoes and a rising sun were displayed on the face. The Legend read "Republica Del Centro de America" in the middle of the coin it will show the Arab number and year of mint.

Decree 4: On the reverse, a tree with the emblem of liberty was shown. At the bottom of the tree the value and number of the coin was given. The inscription around the coin read "libre cresca fecundo". The coin also had the initials of the engraver, place of minting and the number reflecting the silver and gold contents.

Decree 5: In lower value coins of 1 or ½ *reales*, the bust displayed reflect three volcanoes. All others will conformed to the preceding decrees.

Decree 6: In ½ coins no inscription was needed. The bust will content to decree 5. The reverse will have a tree, initials of the engraver, place of minting and year and value of coin

Decree 7: Gold coins will differentiate themselves from silver coins by the placement of the sun being in the middle of the bust.

   The monetary law was pretty short and precise in defining what was needed to mint federal coins. Due to the limited funds and the fact that the Federation had only one mint to depend on, the diversity of the coins was very small.

The Federation produced a total of five different silver coins and five different gold coin denominations.

The silver coin denominations were:

¼ minted between 1824 till 1840 and after the decline of the Federation
½ minted between 1824-1831 and once again after the decline of the Federation
1 minted between 1824-1831 and once again after the decline of the Federation
2 minted between 1825-1832 and once again after the decline of the Federation
8 minted between 1824-1840 and once again after the decline of the Federation

Gold coin denominations were:

½ minted between 1824-1828 and beyond the decline of the Federation
1 minted between 1824-1833 and beyond the decline of the Federation
2 minted between 1825- 1840 and beyond the decline of the Federation
4 minted between 1824-1837 and beyond the decline of the Federation 8 minted between 1824-1837

Guatemala minted the majority of silver and gold coins following the monetary decree of 1824. The state of Honduras started minting coins in 1825. However, the coins minted were of the 1 and 2 *real* variety and were silver coins. Costa Rica minted several gold coins during the period.

Neither Nicaragua nor San Salvador had a mint. However, each state dealt with this problem in different circumstances. For example, Nicaragua participated in various skirmishes, yet it never minted any provincial coins and relied heavily on foreign coins for daily circulation. San Salvador, on the other hand, was generally involved both politically and military in various civil wars and skirmishes. As a result, many expeditions were taken against her; she created the most diverse set of provincial coins in the Federation's existence.

The three traditional volcanoes on the smaller federal coins were a controversial choice, since the seal of the city of Santiago de los Caballeros de Guatemala was chosen to be on them. Many saw this as another attempt by Guatemala to influence the nation.

Seal of the city of Santiago de los Caballeros

<u>Variations and Differences in Records</u>

It must be noted that although the Federation finally sped up the establishments of other mints, the majority of the coins minted were based out of Guatemala. A number of silver and gold coins disappeared from circulation during the various battles around the Guatemalan mint, leading to the production of provincial coins later on.

A few states decided, after the breakup of the Federation, to continue using the designs and monetary value of the federal coins in the late 1840's and 1850's. The following chapters will discuss the various conflicts and the impact on coins of the era. One last note on this topic; there are several coins listed on Krause publications that are very scarce or known. The dates of all known coins, even if only one coin is known are listed in the following chapters.

Chapter 5 Chaos: The Arce Presidency and Civil War

Chapter 5 Chaos: The Arce Presidency

The election of Manuel Arce was a momentous occasion in the history of the republic. President Arce was elected via a compromise with Conservatives in congress. Many Liberal politicians were happy to have one of their own in power, but they felt that Arce would have to compromise to hold power. However, President Arce, surprisingly didn't compromise, he just surrendered power to the Conservatives.

Arce's betray of the Liberal party can be attributed to his greed to hold on to power in a state where Conservatives ruled and provided him with both a large source of income and a military to protect the policies of the administration in power. Tensions rose with the murder of the Liberal governor of Guatemala by religious peasants opposing a more open minded government. The President's inaction convinced many Liberals that he had abandoned the Liberal principles he had sworn to protect. The death of the Guatemalan governor proved to be the last straw for many Liberals. Soon, many states were in open rebellion against Arce's presidency.

The Liberal factions of San Salvador and Honduras decided that congress had failed them and that the President was no longer a Liberal, but a Conservative, and decided to invade the capital to take back power. President Arce quickly gathered the Guatemalan army and a few supporters to stop the invading army. He succeeded and quickly turned to invade his homeland, San Salvador, the base of the Liberal rebellion. This was the start of the first official civil war in the republic's history.

The decision by President Arce to squash Liberals in San Salvador and Honduras doomed him, preventing him from advancing policies in the country. Instead of investing in the infrastructure of the country with the loan obtained from the British bankers, the president, who had received an advance of 300,000 pesos, invested all the money to fight the war. Arce decided that as a general he should lead the army and quickly left his vice president in charge of the government. Clearly, President Arce was more comfortable in the battlefield than in the halls of congress. Using violence and force unfortunately became the norm in Central America for years to come.

The Federal Mints Don't Measure Up

The Federation had been too quick to establish three regional mints. By the time they elected their first president, many problems started surfacing regarding the quality of the coins minted in those mints and whether the country could afford so many mints.

The only mint in good condition and with experience was Guatemala City's mint, established in 1733. The two other mints in, Honduras and Costa Rica were established in 1822 and 1824, respectively, and had little experience in minting coins. Although Honduras had minted several coins during the Iturbide years, most of these coins were of poor quality. Once the coins started circulating in the capital the federal authorities required each mint to come up to standard and suspended them from operating until special equipment could be obtained to improve the quality of the coins.

The provisional silver Honduran and provisional gold Costa Rican coins tilted the tide towards closing the two regional federal mints. Although, both states claimed that the coins produced were minted after the federal mints were approved and were only made to circulate for a period of time, there were other, nationalistic, motives.

Unlike the Honduran silver provisional coins, the gold Costa Rican coins had a different tree on the reverse of the coins. The design was not an accident. The assembly in Costa Rica had decided that the federal coins' reverse would have in place a palm tree instead of the ceiba tree that all federal coins had. The reason was political. The state felt that it needed to retain a part of its identity, and the palm tree had been as recently as 1824 a part of the state's coat of arms. This action by Costa Rica was condemned by the federal congress in 1825 and was seen as a political attack against Guatemala. Although, the Costa Rican assembly didn't apologize, on the contrary they defended the mint's action, the mint was shut down and all federal coins minted after 1830 had the ceiba tree on the reverse.

What would have taken a matter of months took years when Arce's presidency took a more militant stance and when the government was in a state of civil war. The money loaned by the British bankers was used instead to arm the federal army at the expense of public infrastructure, such as the mints.

Ironically, all coins minted by these two mints were placed back in circulation due to a shortage of coins and were very common during the civil war. The first mint to reopen was Costa Rica. This was because Costa Rica had no participation in any civil war battle, due to the political its isolation attributed to its land passage. Thus, when it restarted minting coins in 1828 it was a welcome surprise to the nation that needed new coins. Honduras, on the other hand, was square in the middle of the civil war. It finally restarted minting coins in the 1830's after Morazán had established his government and was investing in the liberal policies of his government.

The Liberal's' Hope: General Francisco Morazán

The invasion by the federal authorities led Governor Prado to issue a call for assistance from the smartest general in the liberal camp: Honduran Francisco Morazán. Francisco Morazán quickly went to the aid of San Salvador. Ironically, on February 14, 1828, President Arce, sensing that the war would come to the capital resigned as president and left Vice President Mariano Beltrana in charge of the country.

The Prado Provincial Coins

The invasion by federal troops on March 17, 1827 officially started the civil war. President Arce took command of the federal army and left the presidency in the hands of vice president Mariano Beltranena. Arce personally ordered the shelling of San Salvador in March 1828.

The Prado provincial coins made their way to Guatemala when General Morazán invaded the state. The coins were used by many of the troops, and merchants had no choice, but to accept them. After the surrender and a Liberal government in Guatemala, the Prado coins were recalled in August and they were reminted into federal coins.

The provisional Prado coins also made their way into Honduras, which was desperate for new coins to enter the market. As a natural ally of the Liberal party, the coins were widely accepted in circulation, and although the coins were of poor quality, the state had no issues with accepting them. Thus, the provincial coins ironically made their way into other federal states and clearly outlined the need for more coins to be in circulation.

Provisional 1828 and 1829 Prado Coins

The Guatemalan State Coin

Morazán successfully invaded San Salvador and aided her in repulsing the federal army. On October 9, 1828, the federal troops surrendered, thus ending the offensive war by the federal government. The next step for General Morazán was to invade Guatemala, which he did in November after the terms of peace were rejected by the Beltrana administration. General Morazán led a 2,000 man army called the United Army Law Protectors and laid siege to the federal capital of Guatemala City.

During the siege of Guatemala, the state government decided that it needed new coins to sustain the economy. In early 1829, the federal mint was converted into the state mint by simply replacing the engraving on the coins. The state was blessed in having the best mint in the country and therefore had no need to create rudimentary provincial coins. A new monetary law was approved in February.

The coins minted by the state were made out of silver, but had the exact same design as the regular federal coins. The coins were only minted in the 1 *real* denomination. The only difference was the legend that instead of reading "Republica De Centro America" it read "Estado de Guatemala". Once the state fell into Liberal hands, though, the coins were reminted into regular federal coins.

On April 12, 1829 the federal government surrendered to General Morazán's army. However, instead of taking over as provincial leader or military ruler he left the decision to congress. The senior Liberal senator Jose Francisco Barrundia was elected president. The new governor of Guatemala was the president's brother, Juan Barrundia.

President Jose Francisco Barrundia

Participation of Other states

The majority of the civil war was fought between the states of: Guatemala, San Salvador, and Honduras. In fact, Costa Rica was the only state not to be bothered by the civil war. It's no wonder that of all the states in the Federation, Costa Rica, would ultimately prove to be the most progressive and stable
in the region.

Nicaragua: A state at War with Itself

It's hard to fathom that there could be two extreme political climates among states during the civil war. However, perfect contrasts were the states of Costa Rica and Nicaragua. While the other states were fighting the civil war, Costa Rica was at peace. Nicaragua, on the other hand, was fighting its own version of the civil war inside its own borders.

The Nicaraguan assembly had taken the civil war more personally than the other states. Unlike the other states, Nicaragua had a long standing feud among its two biggest cities Leon and Managua.

The governor at the time, a Conservative named Manuel Antonio de la Cerda, supported the Arce invasion of San Salvador. His main party base was in the cities of Managua and Rivas. Ironically, the vice governor was a Liberal Juan Arguello, and his party base was in the cities of Leon and Granada. Naturally, the vice governor declared the actions of the chief executive to be illegal. The conflict led to a call to arms among both executives. For the next few years both sides would fight it out until finally General Morazán, after defeating Guatemala sent General Herrera to aid Arguello in squashing the Conservative army.

Throughout the conflict neither side in the war attempted to issue coins. Provincial coins were not issued due to the shortage of funds in the state. Throughout the entire history of the Federation, Nicaragua didn't issue any provisional coins or even a counter stamp. Instead, to sustain her economy Nicaragua relied mainly on foreign coins and the cobs she had minted prior to the existence of the Federation.

Governor Cerda   *Vice Governor Arguello*

Costa Rica: The Peace seeker

The state of Costa Rica was at peace throughout the civil war. In doing so, the state invested its money on new crops like coffee and old crops like dye. It never really believed in having the federal government control its future, and by the beginning of hostilities in 1826 the state was prepared to handle its own affairs. The politicians in Costa Rica waited until 1829 to pass a law, called the Ley Aprilea, which stated that Costa Rica was an independent state free to determine her own destiny until the civil war ended. The timing helped Costa Rica make it known to General Francisco Morazán that until the federal government controlled her sister states it was not to interfere in her affairs. By not declaring her support previously, the state had avoided the civil war reaching her borders. The Ley Aprilea was repealed in 1831 when President Morazán took over the executive office.

Chapter 6: The Liberal Way

President Francisco Morazán

Chapter 6: The Liberal Way

The Liberals take over

Once the Liberal congress met, many of them wanted to punish the Conservatives. Whether these individuals were to be tried or expelled didn't matter, many Liberals simply wanted examples to be made. The harshest penalties included expelling former President Arce and Governor Aynicma from the nation after taxing one third of their estates to help repay the cost of damages to the nation. The strongest punishment came at the expense of the Catholic Church, which was placed under much scrutiny by the federal government for its actions and support of the Conservative party during the war. The archbishop of Guatemala was expelled and so were several other leaders of the Church. Unlike some former federal officials, the Church was not allowed to repay anything; instead its assets were frozen and confiscated by the new government.

The Liberal government went one step further in annulling all previous elections (after 1826) and forcing public officials to return their salaries to the state. These extreme actions led to a rift and renewed rivalry with the Conservatives that led many people to question why they had sided with the Liberals. As soon as Jose Manuel Arce was in Mexico, he started planning his comeback, by force, to the presidency.

1830 Salvadoran Countermark

The state of San Salvador would become the state that would most frequently use provisional and countermarked coins throughout the Federation.

The 1830 countermark was created in order to accept foreign coins that met the federal standards due to shortages of federal coins. Although, the provisional coins were not needed, new coins were, and therefore this small countermark was created with a distinguishing volcano and a double letter s.

One Liberal governor in Salvadoran Juan Maria Cornejo didn't like what was happening with the government in Guatemala and felt that soon the federal government would want more power from the states. When congress moved its headquarters and created a federal district in Sonsonate and ,later San Salvador, Governor Cornejo was outraged and quickly seceded from the Federation. Governor Cornejo also became involved with the exiled President Arce and Archbishop Canas to try to stop Morazán from gaining more power.

To prepare for the new war, Cornejo sensed was coming, he ordered new coins to be minted as provincial in order to fund this war. President Morazán asked for mediation, but the government of San Salvador refused, Morazán had no choice but to invade.

The Cornejo Coins

On January 7, 1832, San Salvador seceded from the Federation all but beginning a new civil war. Ironically, President Morazán felt that the new capital would welcome and strengthen federal influence; however the Salvadoran Governor Jose Maria Cornejo felt that he was being invaded. As a result, he ordered the minting of new provisional coins. These coins would become known as Cornejo coins.

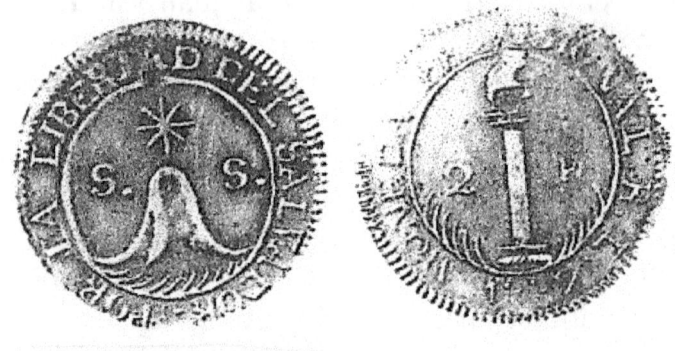

Cornejo Coins

Changes of 1832

The congress that convened in 1832 made some radical changes to the constitution reflecting the liberal policy of the government in power. The two major changes made quite an impact in society at the time, but they would do very little to help the Federation get out of the economic problems they had.

The first law gave the citizens of the Federation the right to worship any religion, thus eliminating the Federation as a Catholic nation. There was no backlash when this law was confirmed. However, later in the decade the Conservatives later in the decade would use it to excite the native Catholics to take arms against Morazán. The second law was to adopt the Livingstone Louisiana Code laws and to adopt trial by jury.

This law was not popular among the masses. It was seen as a foreign law that would support the elite and foreigners in the country at the expense of the poor masses. These two laws were critical to establishing a Liberal government, but the government failed to fully explain to the masses the reasons behind such laws. Conservatives jumped at the opportunity to create fictitious reasons in order to win the support of the masses, especially in rural Guatemala.

Honduras Provisional Coins

San Salvador was not the only Liberal stronghold to have issues with the federal authorities. The state of Honduras under the governorship of Jose Antonio Marquez felt threatened that President Morazán held interest in the state and wanted to make a change in leadership. When Coronel Vicente Dominguez was sent to interfere, the state quickly decided that it needed to speed up her defenses. The creation of the provisional coin would aid the state's need for coins.

The Honduran coins minted bore a resemblance to those minted by Guatemala in 1829. There were only two changes to the legend. The most important was the replacement of the "Republica de Centro America" with "Mon. Provisional del Est. de Hond". The reverse motto was the "Libre Creszca Fecunda T 1832. F". These coins circulated for a few months and were recalled and reminted once a new, friendlier, administration took over the state. The few coins minted have either the 1832 or 1833 date on them.

Cracks in the Liberal Government

President Morazán's invasion of San Salvador was supported by all the states. Ironically, when the president determined he needed to become head of state for San Salvador, the other states not only pulled their support, but seceded from the Federation. At least, they did on paper; in reality no state took steps to establish a separate republic.

This love-hate relationship in congress was not exclusive to the Liberal party, but systematically a problem throughout the entire Federation. It seemed that political parties in the states would give ultimatums when ever no solution could be attained in congress. This game of chicken became the major reason why the Federation was so inconsistent in running the country, regardless of which party was in power.

The New Federal Capital, San Salvador, and the Last Provincial Coins

The federal capital was transferred from Guatemala City to Sonsonate, El Salvador, and a few weeks later on February 5, 1834 to San Salvador. The new capital established a federal district, where the federal government could control all aspects of government.

Naturally, the San Salvadoran government was transferred to another part of the state. This caused great discontent among the government officials in the state, and soon another governor, Joaquin de San Martin started causing problems and President Morazán sacked him. However, the state created another series of provincial coins during this period. These coins would be known as the San Martin provisional coins.

San Martin Provisional Coins and Zig Zag Countermark

The new provisional coins, also known as the San Martin coins, minted by San Salvador were of the 1 *real* denomination only. It was the first time the state's name and seal appeared on the coin. Again, a shortage of coins and problems with the federal government led to their production.

The zig zag countermark was a relatively simple way for the Salvadoran authorities to combat counterfeiters passing on foreign coins in the state. The idea was simple, to have all foreign coins inspected in local government buildings by having an official try to cut down the coins in half with a saw. The result would either show the coins to be of a precious metal, like silver, or of another metal. Those coins that were copper or another material were cut in two. The silver coins would have the mark, and thus be accepted by merchants as legitimate coins.

The Last Federal Elections

President Morazán's popularity had suffered among his Liberal base. However, his Liberal allies in the states, especially Guatemala, had done such a good job at keeping the status quo that Morazán was still a contender to gain reelection. This time Jose Del Valle would win the elections, but ironically, he fell ill and died before he could take office. The great moderate Conservative leader had passed away without ever holding the executive branch of the nation where many saw him as a natural fit. No one ever replaced Valle, thus Morazán won by default. His second, and last, term began on February 2, 1835.

Espinoza Provisional Coins

The last provisional coins minted by San Salvador occurred in 1835 under the leadership of Governor Nicolas Espinoza who felt that the state was not being aided by the federal authorities and decided to mint new provincial coins. The coins minted were all silver and were of the ½ and 1 *real* denominations.

Chapter 7: Cultural Clash: The Decline of the Liberals and the Federation

Chapter 7: Cultural Clash: The Decline of the Liberals and the Federation

The Decline of the Federation

President Morazán was desperate for new funds to balance the federal budget and was trying to levy new tariffs and taxes, but also had a plan to encourage foreign investors to come into the country to invest. In Guatemala, under Governor Galvez, the state had suddenly become the model of liberal policies in the country. From education reforms, to curbing the influence of the Church; the Liberal governor was succeeding in establishing a Liberal haven in Guatemala. He, like the president, encouraged foreign investment and colonization of the most remote parts of the state. However, conservatives with a stronghold among the church elite started spreading rumors that foreigners were going to confiscate the Indian lands to establish British territory, all with the consent of the governor of the state.

Naturally, the peasants felt that it made sense that congress had eliminated the Catholic state so that foreigners, mostly Protestant, would want to take over their land to cultivate it. This led to revolts and riots in several parts of Guatemala by 1835. To make matters worse, a cholera outbreak originating in British Honduras triggered a chain reaction that would bring about the end of the Federation in 1839.

The Ban on Provisional Coins

The federal government had always opposed the states issuing their own coins. Although the majority of the coins minted without the consent of the federal mints had been done to finance that particular state during the civil war. However, states like San Salvador took advantage of the lax federal regulations and it decided to countermark and mint provisional coins to supplement the few federal coins in circulation. In Honduras, the state had been reducing the amount of silver in coins and even minting copper coins due to the terrible economic conditions. Other states, like Costa Rica and Honduras, had previously minted cobs, and even some provisional federal coins, that had led to the federal government to shut them down in order to improve the quality of those coins.

In order to put a stop to this perceived abuse, the federal government passed a new law in 1835 banning the production of all provincial coins and restating the federal government's supreme right to mint coins. Although no new provisional coins were minted, the previous coins continued to circulate and be accepted as coins, due to the shortage of federal coins.

The Beginning of the End

Although there had been various skirmishes in Guatemala over liberal reforms, the governor had a good hold on the various revolts. However, all that would change when cholera cases started to be reported in the countryside in early 1837.

One Last Push

Once the capital was successfully transferred to San Salvador, the president decided it was time to draft new laws to increase revenue in the state coffers. With the help of the British ambassador to Central America and the Caribbean, Frederick Chatfield, the congress drafted new tariff and custom reform laws to not only increase state coffers, but also to end individual state protective tariff laws that had punished colonies like British Honduras. However, the cholera outbreak in Guatemala and the growing hostile tensions by Conservatives made sure that no law would successfully be implemented after 1837.

Ambassador Frederick Chatfield

The outbreak of cholera in British Honduras (Belize) made its way into Guatemala in early 1837. The outbreak had local authorities scrambling for answers on where it originated and how to keep it from spreading to the major cities. Governor Galvez decided to place all medical goods on the table to combat the disease. He sent doctors and nurses to the field, along with military personnel, to help the native Indians treat the disease. However, the reason why the governor sent troops along with the medical staff was not to protect them, but to create quarantines around the infected towns.

A lack of communication and distrust between the Indians and the staff made it impossible for quarantines to be successfully implemented. Most of the Indians feared that they were being discriminated against and isolated from their families for no good cause. The Conservatives charged that the Liberal government was just isolating a political threat and that in fact the government planned to confiscate and later sell those lands to foreigners to encourage investments.

The Church, along with the Conservatives started spreading blatant lies among the Indian population of Guatemala. They claimed that the government had infected the water with poison and that they had caused the problem as an excuse for them to either spread Protestantism (British investors) or kill off the native population so the small, elite population could gain more land. Some rumors involved the economy, such as the rumor that the governor would demonetize the, *real*, and that all federal money would be worthless. Every town was told a different lie, but all of them had the same conclusion; organize against the Liberals and take back the country. As a result of the lies, eventually by 1837, the Guatemalan government was involved in a series of skirmishes that became a short-term civil war in 1838.

The federal authorities were confident that the Guatemalan government could hold on to power and reason would return. However, things took a turn for the worse when the Indian population started following a young man named Rafael Carrera, who became the leader of the Conservative movement. Carrera was an Indian with no education or military experience, however, his personality and his deep commitment to the Church made him a natural leader for the Indians to rally around. Rafael Carrera was not a military genius, but his large numbers of soldiers overwhelmed the most experienced companies of federal troops. The attrition rate helped Carrera ultimately win the war.

Around this time, the highlands of Guatemala, also known as Los Altos, decided it was a perfect time to declare independence from Guatemala and did so on February 2, 1838. The federal government sensing, a disaster in Guatemala and a loss of its Liberal allies, decided to recognize the Liberal government of Los Altos. By late 1838, the governor of Guatemala had fled the state, his troops had been defeated and Rafael Carrera had taken over the state.

President Morazán decided he needed to defeat Carrera in battle in order to keep Guatemala. He led the federal army into Guatemala and made several stands against Carrera's troops. However, Morazán was distracted by events in San Salvador, where congress was meeting to decide the future of the Federation.

Rafael Carrera

On July 20, 1838, the federal congress met to decide the future of the Federation. Many states weren't happy with the proposed taxes and the loss of tariffs in their state. The revolution in Guatemala was spreading to other states, and confidence in the federal government was at an all time low, even among Liberals. Thus, the congress proposed that each state could run a political system of their choosing as long as they remained a part of the Federation. Obviously, this amendment to the constitution made no sense. One could basically, establish a dictatorship in a state and then allow democratic elections to be held for the position of president only. It was a failed amendment and made legal scholars conclude that the Federation was in no position to stop the states from seceding from the union. The president cut his military plans short and returned to San Salvador to try to recall the amendment.

The first state to review the amendment and to actually secede from the union was Nicaragua. On November 5, 1838, the state of Nicaragua declared its independence from the Federation. It was soon followed shortly by Honduras, Costa Rica, and Guatemala. By the time that Morazán's second term came to an end in February 2, 1839, the Federation had all but dissolved.

Francisco Morazán could count only on San Salvador (now he had become governor) and Los Altos for support in rebuilding the Federation. However, Rafael Carrera quickly attacked and overran Los Altos and reintegrated the state into Guatemala. Francisco Morazán was now trapped, he couldn't attack, since he lacked men, he couldn't stay, since others were planning to attack him. Thus he decided that one last military campaign against Guatemala was the only way to regain support from the Liberal base he had always relied on.

Los Altos Coat of Arms

Chapter 8: Coins After the Collapse of the Federation

Chapter 8 Coins After the Collapse of the Federation

When the Federation was declared null in 1838 many states had to rethink their respective state symbols and insignias. Many states assumed that a new union would quickly replace the Federation and continued using the Federation coins even minting them without making many cosmetic changes.

The short-lived state of Los Altos used federal coins, but used a countermark of the quetzal on them. The quetzal would eventually become the national symbol of Guatemala.

This is a summary of what each state did after the collapse of the Federation in order to replace federal coins.

Guatemala: Although it continued minting coins with the federal legend, it started countermarking foreign coins and cob coins to deter fake cobs in 1839.

Los Altos: In its short existence, it used a countermark with the Quetzal to distinguish it from federal coins in 1838.

El Salvador: The former capital of the Federation elected Francisco Morazán as governor. The former federal president allowed the state to import and accept coins of the short lived Peru-Bolivian Federation. However, these coins were countermarked with an 1839 date.

Honduras: It continued to mint federal coins for usage with a difference in the legend of the coins. It permanently replaced the legend with "Moneda Provisional de Estado de Honduras" in 1839.

Nicaragua: No provisional or countermarked coin was used. It continued using all available coins in the region.

Costa Rica: The most prosperous state in the Federation also had the most ambitious agenda when it came to establishing its own coins and its own identity. Governor Carrillo in 1839 passed a decree to mint new Costa Rican coins. Although, Morazán's return to power in 1842 delayed the minting of new coins, by late 1842 the state had the most unique coins in the region. In the meantime, the state instituted in 1841 its first countermark of a six pointed star. Many countermarked coins have a small hole. The countermarked was active for less than a year, only until 1842.

The End of Morazán

The last military campaign by Francisco Morazán was a disaster. Morazán had the superior strategy and the better trained men, but the opposition had too much man power, and that eventually proved to be too much for Morazán. He was defeated in Guatemala City on April 1, 1839. Once he saw the odds were against him, Morazán went into a self -imposed exile in Colombia.

Francisco Morazán returned in 1842 with a new plan to restart the Federation. This time he went to Costa Rica, where he had enough support to overthrow the governor and take over command of the state's militia's. However, Morazán was betrayed and captured in San Jose, Costa Rica, by allied troops. He was quickly court martial and sentenced to death. General Francisco Morazán was executed in San Jose, Costa Rica, on February 12, 1842. His death marked the end of the Federation.

Although the previous states had declared independence from the Federation not one had openly established a republic. Thus, for approximately nine years several attempts were made to reestablish a union or a nation among several states. Not until January 1, 1847, when Guatemala declared it self a republic, did the dream of a union die.

Chapter 9: Legacy of Union

Chapter 9: Legacy of Union

Future Attempts at Union in the Nineteenth Century

Although the Federation had failed and many political actors had played a major role in its downfall, ironically, attempts were made immediately to set up another union. Why? It's hard to understand why the same Liberal and Conservatives leaders that fought each other for decades wanted to again come together as a country. In reality, most states wanted a union without Guatemala as a member. The smaller countries wanted to unite to form an entity that could be as big, in terms of population and land, as Guatemala. Most of the trouble and mistrust always had been directed at Guatemala, so an attempt at union made sense.

Around this time, the British Empire started to pull its weight around British Honduras and saw an opportunity to influence economic policy in the region to benefit its colonies. Many scholars would pin the blame on the British ambassador Frederick Chatfield as the main obstacle to a new union.

Ambassador Chatfield was instrumental in ending the various tariff wars between Guatemala and British Honduras and in securing an understanding with the Morazán government when it came to British investments, including the loan the nation had taken out in 1824. The loan's interest was being repaid, and when the Federation failed, the loan was divided among the five states to pay off the debt. Thus, Britain benefited from Chatfield's negotiations prior to 1840.

However, Chatfield had a change of heart when he saw President Morazán's attempt at forcing taxes on businesses and citizens in 1839 as a danger to British interest. Although, politically independent, he had supported Liberal causes. But the certain collapse of the federation and the aggressive demands of the governors of Jamaica and British Honduras, made him become a political player bend on dividing and stopping any union from coming into existence.

Attempts by the Central American states to come together as a union, whether via legal terms or military force eventually failed.

1842- Former President Francisco Morazán returned from exile to Costa Rica. He successfully overthrew the governor and installed himself as commander. However, he was betrayed by some of his allies and was turned over to the Conservatives who quickly found him guilty of treason and executed him. Morazán's death marked the end of any attempts at restarting the Federation.

1842-1845 Confederacion de Centro America- This pact was created in Chinadega, Nicaragua and established an alliance among El Salvador, Honduras, and Nicaragua. This group elected Juan Jose Canas as a super delegate or leader to lead the confederation. However, this leader never had more power or support from the governors of each state. In reality, he was a figurehead. The confederation disappeared by 1845.

1880-1885 "Intentona de Barrios" Barrios Master Plan- The Guatemalan president Justo Rufios Barrios had taken over his country and had made incredible reforms to modernize the country. His changes included education and monetary reforms. The Liberal agenda had finally taken place in Guatemala and was proving a great success. President Barrios felt it was his duty to spread the wisdom of his ideas throughout Central America. However, he decided that the only way to do so was to organize a new federation, by force, if need be. Barrios' ideas' were opposed by many leaders of the region.

Both the United States and Mexico were against the idea, sensing that his reforms would damage their business interests in the region. Mexico, especially, felt threatened since Barrios had made demands on the border for more land and wanted states like Chiapas returned to Guatemala. Having an armed and progressive Federation under General Barrios was a nightmare for Mexico's President Diaz.

The other states in the region weren't very thrilled about the idea, either. Both Nicaragua and Costa Rica were outraged that Barrios threatened to invade each nation if they refused to convene for a federal congress Barrios wanted. Eventually, Barrios took command of his army and invaded his former ally, El Salvador. President Barrios was killed in action when a bullet hit him in the heart. His death ended the most serious attempt at unification in the nineteenth century.

1895-1898 Republica de America Central- Honduras, El Salvador and Nicaragua signed a new pact in Apala, Honduras. This attempt failed when Salvadoran President Tomas Regalado took over the country and pulled out of the union.

June 1921-January 1922- Central American Federation- A congress was called for all states in the region to meet to discuss creating a new federation. Except for Nicaragua, the states signed an agreement on January 19, 1921 to become a nation. However, this agreement failed to be ratified and the idea was abandoned.

Economic Union Attempts

By the beginning of the twenty century, the concept of union was no longer a reality. If anything, an economic union replaced the idea of a physical union. No longer were threats made against one another, but compromises and free trade agreements among nations ruled the century.

November 14 1907- December 20, 1907- All states agreed to a Central American Court of Justice (CACJ). This alliance lasted until April 1918.

October 14, 1953 Organización de Estados Centroamericanos (ODECA). This group created the common market, a new regional court, Central American bank for integration, and the secretary for economic integration. ODECA lasted until the soccer war between El Salvador and Honduras in 1968.

SICA (Sistema de la Integracion Centro Americana) created on December 13, 1991, to help the region in both economic and security issues. The association added the Dominican Republic as a member state although it's a Caribbean nation. Overall, attempts at unification have been abandoned in favor of economic stability and integration of the region's economies and security apparatus.

Chapter 10 The Legacy of the CAF Designs

Costa Rica

Nicaragua

Honduras

El Salvador

Guatemala/ Los Altos

Chapter 10 The Legacy of the CAF Designs

After the fall of the Federation, many of the Central American nations have commemorative or used the old CAF coin designs in their own nation for either daily use or to commemorative an event. The following breakdown the coins by nation:

Costa Rica

Counter Stamp Coins

The state of Costa Rica continued using the Central American coins for several years after the fall of the federation. However, these coins were counter stamped with the coat of arms and were legal tender within the state. Although, Costa Rica had the most ambitious program within the former Federation to replace coins with their own, it took several years before production was at levels sufficient enough to discontinue using counter-marked CAF coins.

It was, approximately the late 1850's before these coins disappeared from circulation and were replaced with new coins bearing the symbols and design of Costa Rica.

Commemorative Issues

In 1970 the state mint created a gold and silver set to commemorate the attempted unification of Central America. The coins were minted in the denomination of 10 colones for silver and 1000 colones for gold.

Gold Series

These very attractive coins have the bust of the original CAF coins, but with an enhanced sun in the middle and a map of Central America. The reverse has the Costa Rican coat of arms and the typical legend with the date of 1970 and the initials of the regional bank association.

Silver Series

The silver coins have a mixture of the original symbols of the old Federation on the bust, including the original five volcanoes and the ceiba tree in the middle of the volcanoes with the old CAF slogan at the center.

Guatemala

The state of Guatemala continued using the old CAF coins for several years after the fall of the Federation until, it declared its independence and established a republic in 1847. The state used several counter stamps to distinguish it and keep it the market during the 1840's.

Modern Day Issues

The 5 centavo coin design of 1949, which still circulates today, has on the bust the old ceiba tree of the CAF coins along with the Latin slogan. It's the only coin in Guatemala with the old design that is still in circulation.

El Salvador

The state of El Salvador, like the rest of Central America, continued using CAF coins after the fall of Morazán's government. However, it relied mostly on South American and American coins for day-to-day activities.

Commemorative Issues

It wasn't until the eighteenth annual conference of regional central bank governors in 1977 that the nation decided to use CAF designs on her coins. The coins minted were of silver and gold with a denomination of 25 and 250, colones, respectively.

The design of the bust of the coin is the exact reverse of the 1 *real* CAF coins used during the federation's existence, but with the legend stating the eighteenth annual governor's assembly. The reverse of the coin is the coat of arms of El Salvador

Honduras

The birthplace of Francisco Morazán is surprisingly missing in honoring the CAF coins in her numismatic history. Honduras, like the rest of the states, accepted and used CAF coins during the 1840's and after. However, the state never minted a coin with the old CAF design or coat of arms either for daily use or commemorative issue.

Morazán's bust has appeared on many of the nation's coins and paper money, but nothing associated with the old CAF coin design has ever been minted by the state.

Nicaragua

The state with the most problems during the Federation is, ironically, the state that has had more regular issue coins with the old CAF design on them than any other Central American state.

The state of Nicaragua has used the bust of the 1 real coin of the old CAF as the reverse of many of her coins in the twenty century. For example, the silver 1 cordoba coin minted in 1912 had the bust of Spanish explorer Cordoba on the reverse it has the old CAF sun rising over the five volcanoes representing Central America.

Nicaragua used the bust of the old CAF on coins dating from 1912 to as recently as 1974. The coins minted with such symbols were the: 10 centavo, 25 centavo, 50 centavo and 1 cordoba silver coin.

Confederation Issues

In 1899 the Republica de Centro America decided to mint a few issues to show unity among the member states. The coins were minted in France and include a 1 and 5 centavo denomination minted out of copper.

These odd coins show the bust of liberty, very similar in design to the rare gold coins minted by Honduras (at the time the capital of the Republica) and on the reverse, the legend with the denomination of the coin.

These coins are rare in mint condition, but not very expensive in the market for the set. Expect to pay anywhere between $100 and $500 dollars for a great looking set.

1970 Banco Centroamericano Issue

To mark the tenth anniversary of the association of bankers, the association minted a set of silver and gold coins. Both silver and gold coins have a 50 peso denomination. These coins have the exact design of the old 1 real CAF coins on both sides.

The bust shows the sun in the middle of five volcanoes and the legend around celebrating the tenth anniversary. The reverse of the coin has the ceiba tree with the old slogan "libre creza fecundo". The legend around the coin has the association name and the 50 pesos denomination.

This beautiful set of coins is not that rare. You generally see one in mint condition on eBay every few months or at auction. Expect to pay anywhere from $50 dollars for a non-graded silver coin and $500 dollars for a non-graded gold coin.

The Iberoamericana Series

This new series created in partnership between the Spanish and Portuguese mints and several Latin American nations celebrate the historic union between these nations. The two Central American nations participating in the series are Guatemala and Nicaragua. The designs for the series have range from: classic cathedrals, nautical themes, Olympic sports and the newest classic monetary design.

The latest classic monetary design has proven to be a big success with collectors when it was release earlier this year. The theme celebrates the old monetary coin designs many from colonial times. Both Guatemala and Nicaragua integrate classic colonial designs commonly found before independence. The Guatemala design resembles the old classic globe pillar series while Nicaragua displays the classic Central American Federation design of the rising sun on her coins.

Guatemala   Nicaragua

Chapter 11 The Central American Federation Coins

Central America's Central Banks

Chapter 11 The Central American Federation Coins

The coins minted came from the three mints in the Federation. The mints were: Guatemala (G) Costa Rica (CR) and Honduras (H). The majority of coins minted came from Guatemala. However, Costa Rica minted quite a few gold coins during the late 20's and 30's. Most of the coins have a standard uniform look to them; however, a few coins were minted with a different die work and have a more rudimentary look. These are commonly referred to as provincial federal coins. These coins are extremely rare and, as mentioned before were minted by Costa Rica and Honduras mints.

Neither San Salvador nor Nicaragua ever minted official federal coins. However, for a number of years rumors circulated that some federal coins had been minted by Nicaragua because the initials NR appear on these coins. However, these initials indentified the lead assayer at the Honduran mint, Narciso Rosal, who was employed at the mint during the 1820's.

The following dates for coins are those found in the standard Krause Coins of the World catalogs.

¼ *Real*

Years minted: 1824G, 1826G, 1828G, 1831G, 1833G, 1837G, 1838G, and 1840G

½ *Real*

Years Minted 1824G, 1830HO, 1831CR

1 Real

Years Minted: 1824G, 1825, 1828G, 1830Ho and 1831CR

2 Reales

Years Minted: 1825G, 1831H, 1832H

8 Reales

Years Minted: 1824G, 1825G, 1826G, 1827G, 1828G, 1829G, 1830G, 1831G, 1831CR, 1834G, 1835G, 1836G, 1837G, 1839G, 1840G

Gold Series

½ Escudo

Years minted: 1824G, 1825G, 1825CR, 1826G, 1828CR

Escudos

Years Minted: 1824G, 1825G, 1828CR, 1833CR

2 Escudos

Years Minted:1825G,1826G,1827G,1828G,1828CR,1830G, 1834G,1835G,1835CR,   1836G 1837G,1840G

4 Escudos

Years Minted: 1824G, 1825G, 1828CR, 1835CR, 1837CR

8 Escudos

Years Minted: 1824G, 1825G, 1828CR, 1833CR, 1837CR

The gold series of coins is a difficult set to complete. The coins were minted during this time period generally in limited quantities, given the terrible fiscal policies the federal budget had during its existence. The most common gold coins are the smaller denominations of: 1/2 escudo, 1 escudo and 2 escudos. Estimates on these coins range from a few hundred dollars to a few thousand, depending on the grade and condition of the coin.

The rarer 4 and 8 escudos are harder to find in the market. The 8 escudo coin was minted by Guatemala and Costa Rica.

Chapter 12:
Collecting Central American Federation Coins

Chapter 12:
Collecting Central American Federation Coins

The Federation minted several coins in both silver and gold with denominations from ¼ *real* to 8 *reales* from 1824 to 1839. The rarity of each series depends on a variety of issues ranging from what mint it came from to the year minted. Obviously, the higher the denomination of the coins, the rarer they are. Gold coins in near mint condition are especially hard to find.

Here are a few common issues found when collecting these coins:

Holed Coins

A constant problem collector's encounter is that many coins from the era are found in the market with holes in them resulting in a tremendous decrease in value. I have seen many gold pieces with holes in them for chains, and with a great deal of damage to the coins themselves. Why damage a coin? Well, in some respects the hole was a form of countermark (Costa Rica), although in most cases the citizen had decided that the coin would make a better necklace. Although holed coins are very common, they present a golden opportunity to the collector to acquire rare samples that would be out of reach if the coin was in mint condition.

Domestic Countermarks

The counter-marked coins' rarity depends on the state in which it was minted. A few countermarks are not as rare or desirable, such as the Salvadoran zig-zag counter marks. Others, such as the Los Altos quetzal countermark, are extremely rare and sought out.

Foreign coins with countermarks

A major issue with the federal government was its inability to sustain the three mints. It heavily relied on Guatemala to do most of the production and many of the coins minted in Costa Rica didn't circulate in the other states. As a result, states started accepting foreign coins as legal tender, regardless of whether they met the federal standards for coins.

Both state and federal governments passed laws to ban certain foreign coins from circulating due to concerns that these coins had less precious metal content in them. Many foreign coins were countermarked, although they shouldn't have been. For example, the zig-zag countermark used by San Salvador has shown up on American coins of the period.

Fake Countermarks and coins

Counterfeiting has always been an issue for collectors. However, verifying a legitimate countermark on a foreign coin is very difficult. The Krause catalogs and other books on the subject only describe the coins found, so far. Many countermarked coins are rare, and only handfuls have survived. Thus, discovering a new, unique coin that is unlisted in the Krause catalog is possible. However, authenticating these coins is difficult. The coins are legitimate, but are the countermarks? The collector must be well-versed in this field or buy from a legitimate dealer.

Prices for eight *reales* and *escudos*

The most desirable coins to collect are the 8 *reales* in either silver or gold. However, gold 8 *escudos* coins are very difficult to acquire in any condition, and would cost the collector several thousand dollars. The silver *reales* are very commonly found on eBay and at other auction houses throughout the year. Depending on the condition of the coins, the prices can range from a few hundred dollars to a few thousand. In a rare case, Goldberg Auctions sold a rare 8 *real* Costa Rican 1831 coin, graded NGC 63, and claimed to be uncirculated, for a record $21,275.

The 8 *escudo* coin is a very difficult coin to find in mint condition. Coins in less than adequate condition still fetch a four to five figure sum on the open market. The most expensive 8 *escudo* gold coin sold at Heritage Auctions sold for $48,875 in May 2008. A similar specimen from the Guatemalan mint auction of by Goldberg Auctions sold for a record $166,750! These rare graded coins are auctioned off once in a few decades.

Collecting Federal Coins

The unknown legacy of the Central American Federation is a reason why many Central American nations keep` making the same mistakes. A nation at war with itself for the two decades of its existence and with a huge fiscal problem was a nation doomed to fail. The biggest symbol of its existence was its coins, which became its best known symbols after the collapse of the country. The beautiful coins were designed with the hope that the nation would thrive and become a prosperous nation much like the young United States, the nation most of the forefathers of the Federation admired. Sadly, this never happened.

The history of this country is rarely spoken about in contemporary Central American history. Many people seem to conclude that once independence from Spain was achieved, the states formed a union with no purpose, and that eventually they all broke away, and each started its own nation. The only mention of the Federation in contemporary books is generally when referring to Francisco Morazán. A detail study on the nation is scarce. Thus, finding any thorough books on the history of the Federation is like finding a needle in a haystack. A great source is a book published by Bancroft over one hundred years ago!

If finding books on the history of the Federation is difficult, finding one on her coins is almost impossible. There are many dozens of books focusing on specific Central American countries, but not one devoted exclusively to the Federation coins. Perhaps it's the limited number of written records that survive or the lack of interest in the region that makes this era difficult to study for numismatists.

The coins discussed in detail in this book were regular issue coins minted by the Federation. There isn't much data on provisional or cob coins, since many collectors prefer regular issue coins and coins they can acquire. These coins, whether silver or gold specimens, all can be acquired for a few thousand dollars. Of them the gold series is a little bit rarer and more expensive. The limited designs and denominations by the Federation make acquiring a complete set possible.

The majority of these beautiful coins can be collected rather easily if one invests time and money to this goal. The lower denomination coins are not as common on auction sites like eBay, however when they do appear on auction sites they tend to sell for reasonable prices. The higher denomination silver coins are very easily found for sale through various dealers. Many of these coins are not graded and could be damaged. Those coins that are graded tend to be offered for a few hundred dollars. In essence, collecting the silver set seems to be a reasonable and attainable goal.

The real problem in collecting coins from the Federation has been the gold series as these gold coins are very scarce. The Federations had some natural sources for raw materials, including several mines, but the chaotic civil wars never allowed the federal mints to produce adequate gold coins for commerce. The smaller denomination escudos are common enough to find on sites such as eBay and through dealers. The larger denomination coins are very difficult to acquire. The 4 and 8 *escudo* series are not only very rare, but pricy. Naturally, the higher the grade of the gold federal coins the higher the price. Acquiring a complete set from the federal mints is a collector's dream and it is to be hoped, one that many readers will embark on.

Thus, the Federation continues to live in the modern era, thanks to the great coins she minted. The history of these coins has and will continue to keep her memory alive forever.

Bibliography

Almanzar, Alcedo F and Stickney, Brian R. *The coins and paper money of El Salvador*. San Antonio, Almanzar Coins of the World , 1973

Anguiano, Pablo Morales, *Agustin Iturbide*. México City, Grupo Editorial Tono, 2003

Bancroft, Hubert H *History of Central America Vol. III 1801-1887*. San Francisco, The History Company, 1887

Brignoli, Hector Perez, *Breve Historia de Centro America*, Madrid, Alianza Editorial, 1985

Brignoli, Hector Perez *Historia General de Centro America*, San José, FLASCO 1974

Chacon, Hildago and Benito, *Manuel Del Estado a la republica: Las Moneda y la politica de Costa Rica (1821-1850)*. San José. Fundación Museos del Banco Central. 2000

Foster, Lynn V. *A Brief History of Central America* Checkmark Books New York,2007

Guttag, Julius. *The Julius Guttag Collection of Latin America Coins*. New York, Self-Publish 1929

Karnes, Thomas L *The Failure of Union 1824-1975*, Chapel Hill .The University of North Carolina Press 1976

Krause, Chester. *Standard Catalog of World Coins: Spain, Portugal and the New World*. Iowa. Krause Publications 2002

Jara, Carlos *Central America Provisional and Provincial Mint*. Santiago de Chile, Andios Impresos, 2007

Jovel, Roberto J *La Historia Numismática de El Salvador Vol.1* San Salvador 1999

La Politica y las monedas en Centroamerica (1821-1899), San Pedro, Costa Rica:Universidad de Costa Rica 1997.

Mejia, Jose *The Numismatic History of El Salvador*. Los Angeles, Alliance Limited Collectibles, 2011

Prober, Kurt *Historia Numismatica de Guatemala*. Guatemala City, Self Publish, 1973

Robinson, Charles M *The coins of Central America 1733-1965: An illustrated guide to central American coinage* New York, Self Publish 1965

Rodriguez, Mario. *Central America*, New Jersey, Prentice Hall 1965

Schiena, Robert L *Latin America's Wars: the age of the caudillo 1797-1899 Vol.1* Dulles. Brassey's Inc 2003

Smith, Robert S *"Financing the Central American Federation 1821-1838"*. The Hispanic American Historical Review, November 1963 Pg 483-510

Staples, Joan L *Incidents of Travel in Central America, Chiapas and Yucatan*, New York, Doer Publications 1969

Stickney, Brian R *The Coinage and Paper Money of Honduras*. San Antonio, Almanzar Coins of the World, 1981

Stickney, Brian R *The Coinage and Paper Money of Nicaragua*. San Antonio, Almanzar Coins of the World, 1974

Wood, Howland. *The Tegucigalpa Coinage of 1823*. New York, The American Numismatic Society, 1923

Zelaya, Manuel *The History and Coins of Honduras*, Tegucigalpa, Self Publish, 1965

www.ingramcontent.com/pod-product-compliance
Lightning Source LLC
LaVergne TN
LVHW051847080426
835512LV00018B/3111